Dear Ariana 76 years

Happy Reading

Dad

Always love
MOM

THESE WISHES ARE

PRESENTED

WITH LOVE

TO:
_____

FROM:
_____

DATE:
_____

12 Visions of a Mother for Success

A MOTHER'S WISH

*Based on the Seven Life Changing Stories
as Told in "Ancient Secrets of Success
For Today's World"
by Tulshi Sen*

SAMAHRIA RAMSEN

Copyright © 2008 by Samahria Ramsen
A Mother's Wish: 12 Visions of a Mother for Success
by Samahria Ramsen
Printed in Canada, 2008
ISBN 978-0-9699078-7-9
Published by Omnilux Communications Inc.
P.O Box 58101, 3089 Dufferin St. Toronto, ON, Canada,
M6A 3C8

The Seven Life Changing Stories are reprinted with
permission of the Author Tulshi Sen from "Ancient Secrets of
Success for Today's World", ©2005 by Tulshi Sen, Published
by Omnilux Communications Inc. 2006, ISBN 0-9699078-5-0

Library of Congress Cataloguing-in-Publication Data
Ramsen, Samahria

A mother's wish: 12 visions of a mother for success /
Samahria Ramsen
ISBN 978-0-9699078-7-9

1. Parenting--Poetry. 2. Mother and child--Poetry. 3. Success
in children--Poetry. 4. Mothers--Poetry. I. Title.

PS8635.A465M68 2008   C811'.6   C2008-901285-2

Parenting / Self - Help / Success

A little boy snuggled up to his mother
And asked:

"Mother, where did I come from?
Where did you pick me up from?"

The mother hugged the baby
And gave an affectionate smile.
Then she said:

"You were always in my heart."

Rabindranath Tagore
Translated by Tulshi Sen

Dedicated

To

My Daughter, Elina

And My Son, Jacob

I WISH

How can I love my daughter and my son
a little bit more?

How can I make my daughter and my son to smile
a little bit more?

How can I hold my daughter and my son in my arms
and they feel all of my love?

How can I make them more courageous
and not to fear their tomorrows?

This is my quest throughout the day
while I work, cook, clean, shop, and think:

To feel the joy of being a mother without mothering;

To feel the joy of being a teacher without teaching;

To feel the joy of being a friend
without imposing friendship;

To feel the ultimate joy of knowing that my daughter's
and my son's dreams are fulfilled.

I WISH

MY CHILDREN TO BE SUCCESSFUL

THE UNIVERSE BOWS TO A MOTHER

The Author's Note

It is a wish of every mother to see her child as someone Special. Every mother dreams that one day she will be recognized as a mother of a great woman or of a great man. This is the reward of Motherhood.

A wish for a child's success is in every mother's heart. A Mother's Wish will always come true. It is said that even the Universe bows to a Mother, for she is the heartbeat of the Universe itself. She is the carrier of life.

As Mother-Earth, which gives her body to nurture every seed and every blade of grass, a mother gives her body to nurture and strengthen her child's character and soul.

Before a child comes, a mother dreams great dreams for her child. And a child's birth is the manifestation of a mother's dream.

She waits each day for that holy event. She anticipates each moment. She feels each movement. She cherishes this joyful pain, the sweetest pain of all – the birth of her child.

Along with many of you, I also remember that moment. It was surreal. It was magical. It was euphoric.

I remember silently pressing my baby girl to my bosom and quenching her first earthly thirst. Holding my daughter in my arms for the first time, I whispered in silence: you are Invincible. You are the epitome of Beauty. You are the Universe. You are the poetry of my Life.

Later on I described my feelings of that moment in "A Mother's Love Song for a Daughter".

Along with many of you, I also wish that the power of my love will override all the negative forces and bring peace, harmony, and prosperity into my daughter's and my son's lives. I vision, and I pray…

I bless them to be confident and to attract into their lives all that they love, and all that they deeply cherish in their hearts.

In Strength, Serenity, and Success,
Samahria Ramsen, a Mother

WE ARE ALL - A CHILD OF A MOTHER

We Are All –
The Carriers of the Torch of Life

A mother's love is like the moon, the reflected love of the Creator. She sees her new born, a toddler, and wonders, what her little one is going to be.

A mother of today's world knows that her child has to be strong to face the uncertainties of our time. It is not going to go away. It is here now. And it is increasing as you read these words.

When I was in school, I could decide, what I wanted to be, do, and have. In today's world, where distance is dead and speed wins, it is different.

Children of today's rapidly shifting world have to be given special guidance to combat these inevitable uncertainties. So they can vision what they want to be and do, regardless of what their circumstances and conditions are.

12 Visions of a Mother for Success, dormant or awakened, are latent in the heart of every mother.

If they are already awakened, this book will reinforce the power that is already in the mother. And it will inspire the mother to whisper the power into her child's soul; no matter if her daughter or her son is still a child or a middle aged woman or man.

If these Visions are latent, this book will awaken the mother to the visions. And she will bless her child to embrace these grand possibilities and face the challenge of being a Success.

Mother's blessings never fail. We know it. We are all - a child of a mother. We are all - the carriers of the torch of life.

A Mother's Blessings for Success are the affirmations to remind us of our identity and our purpose in life and to help us overcome stress and uncertainty of our time.

We will be a Success.

THE CRADLE OF LEADERSHIP

*A Leader's Character
Is Determined by the Honour, Dignity, and
Respect They Give to Their Mothers*

Leadership begins in the cradle
Every mother wants her child to grow up to be a leader.

It starts with the lullabies of the mother. It starts with the stories she puts her baby to sleep with. It starts with the embrace the child wakes up to.

She continuously blesses her child, while she follows her profession, bakes cookies, does laundry, or goes grocery shopping.

The heartbeat of a mother is the first piece of music that a child listens to.

The **affectionate look of the mother** is the first experience of love that a child immerses in.

A mother is the first teacher and the first love of a child. Wherever the child may be, the mother is in the child's heart.

A child grows up, develops a character, and becomes a leader; and carries on these mother's Visions, implanted in his or her heart.

A Leader's character is determined by the honour, dignity, and respect they give to their mothers. And this honor, dignity, and respect are always unconditional.

A mother is the source of a child's inspiration to find their purpose in life.

12 Visions of a Mother for Success will give the child the pattern for the foundation of success.

Then we will live a life of Bliss.
That is a Mother's Wish.

TEACHING TOOLS
OF A MOTHER

The Storehouse of Knowledge and Wisdom

Since the beginning of motherhood mothers have told us stories to teach us. Stories are the storehouse of knowledge and wisdom. The bards, the sages, the great leaders, and teachers have passed on their wisdom to us through stories.

Sometimes these stories are called parables; and sometimes they are called epics. Stories enlarge life and breathe inspiration into our hearts. They expand and strengthen our greatest faculty, our Imagination.

We cannot conceive of a life without stories. Every life is a story. Stories have moved people from the depth of depression to the heights of conquests.

It is the mother's voice that transforms stories into the nectar of life, which we drink and quench our thirst with for more and more life.

Mother's stories become movies in our mind and hearts. We replay these movies throughout our life and then pass them on to our children.

Some stories engage all our five senses and stay in our memory banks to guide us through our daily life.

I grew up with stories. I was lulled to sleep and was awakened with stories my mother told me or sung to me with her melodic voice.

And I still hear the echoes of her songs and her stories in my heart, and feel the warmth of her affectionate blessings. She was the one, who had opened for me the door into the world of imagination with no beginning or ending.

Today I am a mother myself. I raised my children with the same stories that empowered me; and guided them from the cradle to the boardroom. These stories were the vehicle to plant into my daughter's and my son's hearts the principles of success.

Seedlings of Success

"A Mother's Wish" was composed by me a long time ago as a gift to my son and my daughter. My original composition was in the form of Inspirational Posters: "A Mother's Prayer for a Son and a Daughter" and "A Mother's Love Song for a Daughter and a Son" to be hung in their rooms and offices.

Then, not long ago, I came across the book that completely changed my own world. The name of this book is "Ancient Secrets of Success for Today's World" by Tulshi Sen.

Being an author of four inspirational books myself, I was grateful and humbled by my experience. I realized that all my life I have lived these teachings. I could not resist the message of "Ancient Secrets of Success for Today's World".

It seemed to me that all the truth that I had found before was distilled in this book to be realized by any one who has the desire to be successful.

This book has seven stories. These stories alone, can take a man or a woman from their lowest point of life to the pinnacle of success, if they just absorb them.

These stories are ancient folklore. They had been told a thousand times over the centuries; but the way they were re-told by Tulshi Sen, makes the mind bow to the principles of life; and allows the wisdom to enter into the heart.

I also realized that I could offer these Seven Life Changing Stories, as told in "Ancient Secrets of Success for Today's World" by Tulshi Sen, to mothers from the mother's point of view.

I did not want to interpret these stories and take away the power that captured my heart the way the Author has exposed these stories.

For the benefit of the reader, and with the gracious permission of the Author, Tulshi Sen, I have included these Seven Life Changing Stories at the end of this small volume.

With joy and the enchantment of a mother I present to you, who are mothers, and to sons and daughters, *A Mother's Wish, 12 Visions of a Mother for Success,* to live a magical and a happy life.

The yardstick of success is not measured
By fame and wealth;

It is measured by your level
Of understanding of who you are,

Why you are here,
And where are you going from here.

Your measure of your success
Is your own happiness quotient.

---Tulshi Sen

THE FIRST

MOTHER'S WISH
FOR
SUCCESS

***

Know Who You Are;

Why Are You Here;

*And Where Are You
Going From Here.*

Your personal Identity
Is like a whirlpool
In the Ocean of Consciousness.

---Tulshi Sen

MEDITATION

The Purpose: The First Meditation will make you recognize who you are; identify that all the power of the Universe is in you; and understand that your every desire is a promise.

The Method: Invest ten minutes every day to meditate alone in a quiet place. Let go of everything you know. Empty your mind. Let Serenity and Peace enter your being.

The Practice: Ask yourself:

Who is this I? Where did I come from? Where am I going from here?

Just listen. Do not answer. Keep listening. Your intellect does not know the answer. Listen to your heart.

*** Remind yourself throughout the day:

I don't need to go outside myself for anything I want. I am Perfect and I am Whole.

I live under the shade of the Wish Fulfilling Tree. Consciousness is my total supply. **Strength, Serenity, and Success is My Banner and My Shield.**

THE SECOND

MOTHER'S WISH
FOR
SUCCESS

***

Walk on Earth
Lightly but firmly;

Do not carry
Any excess baggage of
Guilt, greed, and fear,

But only the wisdom
Of your experiences.

We must release ourselves
From this self imposed dream
That surrounds us at this moment,
And form a Vision of the reality
That we truly desire.

---Tulshi Sen

MEDITATION

The Purpose: The Second Meditation will help you to make peace with your past and confidently build the Vision of your future.

The Method: Invest ten minutes every day to meditate alone in a quiet place. Let go of everything you know. Empty your mind. Let Serenity and Peace enter your being.

The Practice: Say to yourself:

I Walk on Earth lightly but firmly; I do not carry any excess baggage of guilt, greed, and fear, but only the wisdom of my experiences.

I thank my past for teaching me, how to live in the present; and for transporting me in the future now.

I have no regrets. I have made peace with my past. I am invincible. Nothing can harm me.

*** Remind yourself throughout the day:

I am free. I walk erect, lightly but firmly. I radiate light and beauty. My presence inspires and heals.

I love my life. Strength, Serenity, and Success is My Banner and My Shield.

THE THIRD

MOTHER'S WISH
FOR
SUCCESS

***

Your Dignity
Shall be your highest Possession;

And your Confidence
Shall never be used
For Vengeance.

Without Dignity
All the wealth of the world
Is a beggar's bowl, filled with riches.

The weak seek vengeance.
The strong forgive and move on;
And never look back.

---Tulshi Sen

MEDITATION

The Purpose: The Third Meditation reinforces self-esteem. Success is directly proportional to self-esteem. Self-esteem obliterates the need for Vengeance and redirects the wasted energy of vengeance to self-growth.

The Method: Invest ten minutes every day to meditate alone in a quiet place. Let go of everything you know. Empty your mind. Let Serenity and Peace enter your being.

The Practice: Say to yourself:

My Dignity is my highest possession. I shall never use my Confidence for Vengeance.

I respect myself. My Dignity and Confidence are the two wings that make me fly.

*** Remind yourself throughout the day:

I shall not misuse the power that I possess. I know, "He, who lives by the sword, shall perish by the sword."

I know that I cannot fail. Strength, Serenity, and Success is My Banner and My Shield.

THE FOURTH

MOTHER'S WISH
FOR
SUCCESS

***

Hold your head above
Where the eagles soar,

And yet your feet
Grounded on the earth.

Thinking big and thinking small
Takes the same effort;
So, why think small?

---Tulshi Sen

MEDITATION

The Purpose: The Fourth Meditation will help you to stay balanced on your path to success.

The Method: Invest ten minutes every day to meditate alone in a quiet place. Let go of everything you know. Empty your mind. Let Serenity and Peace enter your being.

The Practice: Say to yourself:

I shall hold my head above where the eagles soar, and yet my feet shall be grounded on the Earth.

I recognize my equality with every one. I can rub shoulders with kings and commoners with equal comfort.

I have a beautiful demeanor. I control my emotions. The more balanced I feel, the more successful I become.

*** Remind yourself throughout the day:

My thoughts, words, and actions create or destroy my sense of balance. I do not allow negative thoughts and negative people into my world.

I direct my thoughts and watch my actions. I stay centered. I keep my balance. Strength, Serenity, and Success is My Banner and My Shield.

THE FIFTH

MOTHER'S WISH
FOR
SUCCESS

***

*Do not measure
Your power and greatness*

*By your Fortune,
But by your Virtue.*

Wealth without virtue
Is like having an exotic palace
On a toxic land.

---Tulshi Sen

MEDITATION

The Purpose: The Fifth Meditation helps us to realize that wealth comes from virtue. Virtue is the power of the individual, which generates success.

Patience and calmness, fortitude and self-reliance, courage and humility are key virtues among many other virtues. They are the measure of true success.

The Method: Invest ten minutes every day to meditate alone in a quiet place. Let go of everything you know. Empty your mind. Let Serenity and Peace enter your being.

The Practice: Say to yourself:

I shall not measure my power and greatness by my fortune, but by my virtue.

I love my life. I take control of my actions by cultivating patience. I practice expectation of what I desire. All I want is already mine.

*** Remind yourself throughout the day:

I am patient - I can wait. I am confident - I can command.

I attract what I most desire. Strength, Serenity, and Success is My Banner and My Shield.

THE SIXTH

MOTHER'S WISH
FOR
SUCCESS

***

Be Rich;

But also know

That penniless
You still can own the world.

Your Consciousness
Is a Touchstone.
And it can make gold at will.

---Tulshi Sen

MEDITATION

The Purpose: The Sixth Meditation takes away the fear of lack and develops confidence in the Law of Attraction for the pursuit of wealth accompanied with happiness.

The Method: Invest ten minutes every day to meditate alone in a quiet place. Let go of everything you know. Empty your mind. Let Serenity and Peace enter your being.

The Practice: Say to yourself:

- *I am rich. And I also know that penniless I still can own the world.*

There is abundance everywhere I look. I scoop abundance from abundance; yet abundance never ends.

I carefully watch the flow of my thoughts. My thoughts create what I desire; and bring to existence what does not exist. I am rich. I own my World.

*** Remind yourself throughout the day:

I am one with the source of my happiness and riches. I attract all that I desire.

I attract all that I love. Strength, Serenity, and Success is my Banner and my Shield.

THE SEVENTH

MOTHER'S WISH
FOR
SUCCESS

***

Be Successful;
But also Realize

That your Success
Is rooted in your Faith.

Faith fizzles Fear.

---Tulshi Sen

MEDITATION

The Purpose: The Seventh Meditation reinforces the power of Faith as the source of your strength.

It makes you realize who you are; and where you come from.

The Method: Invest ten minutes every day to meditate alone in a quiet place. Let go of everything you know. Empty your mind. Let Serenity and Peace enter your being.

The Practice: Say to yourself:

My success is rooted in my Faith. I have faith. I am successful.

I increase my success with faith. My faith creates my world.

I know that I do nothing of myself. I have discovered the Universe of limitless supply, adventure, and love. All my desires are fulfilled.

*** Remind yourself throughout the day:

Nothing stands between me and my faith. I am invincible. I feel secure and peaceful. I attract what I accept as mine.

I live under the shade of the Wish Fulfilling Tree. Strength, Serenity, and Success is My Banner and My Shield.

THE EIGHTH

MOTHER'S WISH
FOR
SUCCESS

***

Do not allow yourself the Luxury of dwelling in Fear;

Make your fear the founding stone of your Success.

Does Fear and Pain
Bury you,
Inspire you, or
Goad you forward?

---Tulshi Sen

MEDITATION

The Purpose: The Eighth Meditation helps you transmute Fear into Power.

The Method: Invest ten minutes every day to meditate alone in a quiet place. Let go of everything you know. Empty your mind. Let Serenity and Peace enter your being.

The Practice: Say to yourself:

I use all my power to make my fear into the founding stone of my Success.

I know that fear is a warning signal for me to guard my thoughts. I close my mind to all evil, to all limitations, and to all disease.

I face all my challenges as blessings to be converted into success. I direct my attention to plenty. I think of Abundance. I Live and let Live.

*** Remind yourself throughout the day:

Like the Phoenix, I rise from my own ashes.

I build my success on the pillar of my past failures. Strength, Serenity, and Success is My Banner and My Shield.

THE NINTH

MOTHER'S WISH
FOR
SUCCESS

***

Be Light;

Laugh at yourself;
See through Things;

And also enjoy Things
The way they are.

I laugh at myself,
When I realize that I take living too seriously.
I came with nothing.
What am I clinging on to now?

---Tulshi Sen

MEDITATION

The Purpose: The Ninth Meditation will help you to lighten up, to see the beauty in every moment, and to live fully.

The Method: Invest ten minutes every day to meditate alone in a quiet place. Let go of everything you know. Empty your mind. Let Serenity and Peace enter your being.

The Practice: Say to yourself:

I laugh at myself. I see through Things. And I also enjoy Things the way they are.

My life is laughter and joy. My laughter lightens my heart and ignites images of delight.

My every moment is a perfect moment, for I created it by my own past deeds. This moment is my possession. I earned it.

*** Remind yourself throughout the day:

I do not take life too seriously. I laugh at my mistakes, for there are no mistakes in my life. I enjoy things as they are.

I love my life. Strength, Serenity, and Success is My Banner and My Shield.

THE TENTH

MOTHER'S WISH
FOR
SUCCESS

***

Let your Intellect
Be your Compass;

But let your Heart
Be the Guide to set the Mark.

Set Your Mark High.
Go Beyond Your Intellectual Capacity.
Just Imagine…

---Tulshi Sen

MEDITATION

The Purpose: The Tenth Meditation will help you to vision beyond your intellectual capacity; and go where you have never gone before.

The Method: Invest ten minutes every day to meditate alone in a quiet place. Let go of everything you know. Empty your mind. Let Serenity and Peace enter your being.

The Practice: Say to yourself:

My Intellect is my Compass. My Heart is my Guide to set the Mark.

I dream impossible dreams. My heart guides me. I go where I have never gone before.

I command my intellect to be my compass and point me to the direction I want to go.

I am the captain of my ship. I set my own destination, regardless of my circumstances.

*** Remind yourself throughout the day:

My heart sets the goal. My mind, my intellect, and my body take me to my goal.

I go where I have never gone before. Strength, Serenity, and Success is My Banner and My Shield.

THE ELEVENTH

MOTHER'S WISH
FOR
SUCCESS

***

Be balanced
In pain and pleasure;

Know
That there is always
One more step to be taken.

The two monsters,
Which want to devour us,
Are Too Much and Too Little.

---Tulshi Sen

MEDITATION

The Purpose: The Eleventh Meditation will make you realize that the unknown is the root cause of all fears.

You will know that there is no end; that there is always one more step to be taken.

The Method: Invest ten minutes every day to meditate alone in a quiet place. Let go of everything you know. Empty your mind. Let Serenity and Peace enter your being.

The Practice: Say to yourself:

I am balanced in pain and pleasure. I know there is always one more step to be taken.

I regard my pain and my pleasure as the steering wheel that takes me forward on my journey of life.

When pain strikes me, I am not afraid. When pleasure invades me, I am not conquered by it. I keep on balancing by taking one more step forward.

*** Remind yourself throughout the day:

I am even in pain and pleasure.

I know there is always one more step to be taken towards my highest goal. Strength, Serenity, and Success is My Banner and My Shield.

THE TWELVTH

MOTHER'S WISH
FOR
SUCCESS

***

Be
An invincible warrior

Whose secret weapon is
Love.

The Purpose of Life is Love.

---Tulshi Sen

MEDITATION

The Purpose: The Twelfth Meditation makes you realize that the Divine Weapon is Love.

With love we can conquer our world.

The Method: Invest ten minutes every day to meditate alone in a quiet place. Let go of everything you know. Empty your mind. Let Serenity and Peace enter your being.

The Practice: Say to yourself:

I am an invincible warrior. My secret weapon is Love.

I destroy all negativity and pain of my life with love. My love is to give happiness to myself and others.

When I love, I am fearless.

*** Remind yourself throughout the day:

I am an Invincible Warrior. My only weapon is Love, for "Love never faileth."

Strength, Serenity, and Success is My Banner and My Shield.

GRATITUDE

OF
A MOTHER

***

I am blessed
To be a Mother.

Thank You, My Lord,
Thank You.

FOR GROWN UP KIDS AND KIDS

The Seven Life Changing Stories

From

ANCIENT SECRETS
OF SUCCESS
FOR
TODAY'S WORLD

By Tulshi Sen

LIFE
IS
A TOUCHSTONE

The Story of How Success is Rejected

Once upon a time in a small village in a Himalayan valley lived a poor storekeeper. His store was the only store in this remote, isolated village far away from any town. The village was poor and so was the storekeeper.

A great Master was passing through the village and needed to stay there for three days. The poor storekeeper invited the Master to stay with him. The Master was pleased and the storekeeper, with the little he had, made the Master comfortable in his home as far as he could.

At the end of the three days when the Master was taking

leave, the storekeeper fell at the feet of the Master and asked him for his blessings.

He said, "Master, please bless me that I can be rich. You yourself see now that the income from my store is not sufficient to support me and that my house is a hovel."

The Master blessed him and said, "I will do better than that. I will give you this stone and this stone is no ordinary stone. If you touch iron to this stone, the iron will instantly turn into gold. And by the way, I will leave this stone with you for the next three months. When I will be returning from my pilgrimage in three months from now, I will take back this stone from you. You have three months to make yourself rich; as rich as you want to be."

The poor storekeeper was ecstatic and thanked the Master profusely. The Master continued on his journey.

The village was located in a very remote and a very isolated valley in the Himalayas. The nearest town was far away and the only way to get there was to trek through the mountains on foot. In that town a bazaar was held once a month and only once a month. In that bazaar there was only one iron merchant.

On the day of the bazaar of the first month the poor storekeeper made the long trek to the town, excited to become rich and live a very happy, luxurious life. The promise of the future hummed before him.

He straight away went to the iron store and asked the merchant the price of iron. The iron merchant told him the price of iron was going up and now it was nine Rupees for forty kilos. This enraged the poor storekeeper.

In his anger he said, "I am nobody's fool. You are into profiteering; I will not let you have the satisfaction of fooling me. I will come back next month and then you will come to your senses and sell me the iron at the right price." The storekeeper stomped out, still poor. Little did he realize how much just one kilo of gold would do to his poverty struck life.

Next month, the still poor storekeeper made his way to the bazaar. As he was approaching the iron merchant, he felt a sense of anger overwhelming him. The iron merchant saw him and said, "You should have bought your iron last month; the price has doubled and now it is eighteen Rupees for forty kilos." The iron merchant gave him half a smile.

This infuriated the poor storekeeper even further and he felt that the iron merchant knew that he was desperate to buy the iron. He was not going to give the merchant the satisfaction of taking advantage of him. He also thought that if he held out for another month the merchant would buckle under and give him a fair price.

He said to the iron merchant, "I understand that you know how much I want to buy the iron, but you don't know that I am not a fool. I can wait it out. I will come back next month and then you will have no choice but to sell me the iron at the right price."

The day of the bazaar of the third month arrived and the still very poor storekeeper, with the anticipation of becoming rich, made his way to the marketplace. He asked the iron merchant, "You had a whole month to think. Are you ready to be fair and give me a fair price for your iron? I intend to buy all your iron."

The merchant said, "I always offered you a fair price. I am sorry I have to disappoint you again. Now the price has gone up by another nine Rupees and now it is twenty seven Rupees for forty kilos." The merchant laughed and continued, "You should have bought it the first month you came."

This enraged the poor storekeeper. He totally lost his balance and walked out of the store saying, "Under no circumstances am I going to let you have the better of me." In his numbness of anguish, in his total immersion of living the mundane life, he became oblivious to the fact that he had now had the Touchstone for almost three months. And that this was his last month with the touchstone and this was the last market day to get the iron.

In the meantime the Master finished his journey and remembered the poor storekeeper and his Touchstone. He also remembered that he had to pick up his Touchstone. As he entered the village he was looking for a well lit up store and all the signs of plenty and affluence. He could not find the store he was expecting to see, as he was still looking at the hovel.

The storekeeper saw the Master and came running to him with folded hands and greeted him.

The Master asked, "What happened? Why are you not rich already? Did you not find iron in the bazaar?"

The poor storekeeper replied, "Oh great Master, yes there was plenty of iron but the iron merchant kept raising the price on me. I could not let him have the better of me."

The Master said, "That is good but I must be on my way and I have come to collect my stone from you as your three months are over."

The poor storekeeper gave him back the stone and the Master continued his return journey. The poor storekeeper remained poor.

Our Consciousness is our Touchstone. The three months are the three periods of our life, which are youth, middle age, and senior years. Then the Touchstone will be taken away by the Great Master. What we do with it during these three months is up to us.

THE STORY
OF THE
WISH FULFILLING TREE

How to Guard the Self-Sabotaging Mind

In a small village far away from anywhere and with no access road to the nearest town lived a poor Farmer. He had nobody. No family to help him to farm. He was all alone.

In the heat of a scorching summer's day he had to go to town to buy seeds for his next crop. He had to walk there while the sun beat down on the parched earth and on him. It was hot.

Half way to town the Farmer saw a beautiful Tree with long and strong branches, still filled with green luscious leaves. Under the Tree at the base of the trunk it was cool and the shade defiantly challenged the scorching Sun. He decided to rest there for a while.

As he was dozing off in the cool of the shade resting under the Tree he thought if he would have a cold glass of water it would be great. He did not realize that he was sitting under a Wish Fulfilling Tree. Before you know it, he saw a very cold and refreshing glass of water before him. He quenched his thirst and wished if only he could have some sweets and some food. Lo and behold he saw a banquet before him.

After having had the meal of his life he wished, if only he would have a bed to take a nap. He was lying on a most comfortable bed before he could even speak his thought out completely. He immediately thought if only he had a house to sleep in on this comfortable bed and the house was there before you know it.
The fulfillment of one wish led to larger and larger wishes. Before you know, he had wanted the most beautiful woman for a wife and had plenty of children to help him in the farm, and there he was surrounded by family and wealth.

When he saw what he got just by wishing; he got a little

worried. No, as a matter of fact he got a lot worried. He thought, "What will happen if now a ferocious man eating tiger comes out of the jungle and eats me up?"

A ferocious man eating tiger appeared and ate him up. He was still sitting under the Wish Fulfilling Tree.

We live and move and have our Being under the Wish Fulfilling Tree. This Tree is our Consciousness, the individualized Cosmic Consciousness. The same Power that created this magnificent Universe which cannot be comprehended by our mind, let alone by our brains. This Power works without question or pause and will not judge your wishes, it will fulfill them instantly.

Everything, every circumstance and every condition in your life whether in the past or in the moment was brought to you by your thoughts from this Wish Fulfilling Tree.

THE STORY OF THE FROG
OF THE WELL
AND THE FROG
OF THE OCEAN

How We Form Limitations
And Break Free From Limitations

Once upon a time a crane caught a frog from the ocean and was taking it to its babies for dinner. As the crane was flying over a well, the frog struggled out of the beak of the crane and fell into the well. It was a shocker for the frog of the ocean when he plunged into the deep well.

After he recovered and came to his senses he saw that a

strange frog, sitting on a floating log of wood, was staring at him. The frog of the well asked him, "Where did you come from?"

"From the Ocean," said the frog of the Ocean.

"How big is the Ocean?" asked the frog of the well.

The frog of the Ocean did not want to tell him the size of the Ocean, as he felt that the frog of the well would not be able to understand the immensity of his world. He just kept silent.

The frog of the well thought that either the frog of the Ocean was suffering from a shock from the plunge he took or he was shocked at the size of his huge well. The frog of the well had never ever seen any other place in the Universe. The little well was his world. For him nothing else could be bigger. That was his belief.

So he said to the frog of the Ocean, "Look! Make yourself comfortable; there is plenty of room here just on this log of wood. You take the other end, and I will continue to live where I am living."

The frog of the Ocean thanked him and took up his new residence.

The frog of the well couldn't help himself and his curiosity got the better of him. He asked, "Tell me how big this place that you come from is? Is it half the size of this well?" He was sarcastic and was trying to be painfully funny.

The frog of the Ocean still kept silent. He knew that it was not possible to make the frog of the well believe that there were other worlds, and that they were far too big for his comprehension. He also knew that if he did tell him, he would not be able to prove it to him as there was no way out of this little well, the world of the this little frog. He could not take him to the Ocean.

The frog of the well would not give up. He insisted on finding out from the frog of the Ocean the size of his world and kept on asking him.

Finally one day the frog of the Ocean, caught off guard by the frog of the well, broke his silence and said, "The Ocean is infinite. If all the wells like this one were put in the Ocean they would get lost in the Ocean." After saying this, the frog of the Ocean realized that he had broken his silence and made himself stand foolish in front of ignorance.

The frog of the well did not know whether to laugh or to cry that he now was destined to live with a raving mad frog. He humored the frog of the Ocean and mourned for himself.

He said to the frog of the Ocean, "Don't worry, everything will be okay for you; once the shock of the plunge you took into the well...right from the jaws of death...has worn off."

The frog of the Ocean returned to his silence. The frog of the well started to take care of the frog of the Ocean and expected to heal him of his mental disorder.

It so happened that in that region there was a big ferocious flood and all the wells overflowed. The two frogs found themselves out of the well. The frog of the Ocean knew his way home to the Ocean. He took his forced companion, the frog of the well, and showed him the Ocean. The frog of the well saw a new world. His mind expanded and became the Ocean. He too became silent.

THE STORY
OF THE SCORPION
AND THE FROG

How We Sting Success
When it Stares Us in the Face

On a bank of a river lived a Scorpion and a Frog. The Scorpion wanted to cross the river. He could not swim. He asked the Frog to give him a ride on his back and take him to the other bank.

The Frog instinctively said, "I would love to help you out. But you see I can't, because you see when I put you on my back you will sting me and I will die."

The Scorpion laughed and replied, "Don't be silly. Don't you have any sense? I am smart and I also want to live.

If I sting you and you die, I will drown and die too. You know that I can't swim."

The Frog was convinced. He took the Scorpion on his back and started to swim towards the other side of the river. As they came to the middle of the river the Scorpion forgot his purpose because his instincts overpowered him. He forgot about his own safety. His urge to sting started to intensify, and he was aching to sting. He could not help himself. He forgot about his goal to cross the river. He lost control over himself and stung the Frog.

The Frog looked up and said, "What did you do? Why did you sting me? Don't you realize that now we are both going to die?"

The Scorpion replied, "I lost control. My habit had the better of me but I know that it is too late now."
The Frog and the Scorpion died.

The Scorpion is our mind and intellect, and the Frog is our Consciousness. Our Consciousness creates and takes us to the goal set by the mind and intellect. The same mind and intellect sabotages the process with the sting of negative thoughts, thoughts of dependency on conditions and circumstances. We don't seem to let our Consciousness take us to our destination.

The Masters knew the sting of the Scorpion was fatal to the Scorpion itself. They formulated a system with which the Scorpion can control his instincts and cross the river. Part Two will lead the reader through this process of controlling the sting of negative thoughts.

THE STORY
OF THE LION CUB
WHO WAS RAISED
BY GOATS

*How We Deny Our Identity
And Stay Ordinary*

One day a hunter killed a lioness and dragged it away. He did not know that she had a cub in the cave, and left it there. The cub was helpless. There were some goats around who felt for the lion cub, and brought up this cub as one of their own.

The Lion cub grew up eating what the goats ate, it thought what the goats thought, it bleated as the goats bleated and it lived as a goat. It did not know anything better. It was happy and contented and scared of everything and survived on grass and leaves.

Then one glorious day a magnificent lion appeared on a hillock around where the goats were grazing and gave a loud roar. All the goats ran helter-skelter. The lion cub did not run. He felt a sense of kinship but did not know what it was. The cub looked up in amazement at this regal powerhouse, and stood still. The Lion walked up to the cub and said, "Who are you? Where is your mother? And why do you eat grass and leaves?"

The slightly scared lion cub feeling a sense of frightened joy bleated, "I am a goat. These goats are my family. What else can I eat?"

The Lion roared with dismay and said, "You are a Lion and you eat meat and not grass. Grass is for goats. And don't bleat, you roar." The Lion gave a roar again and the whole forest reverberated with the sound.

The lion cub bleated back and said, "No, I'm a goat. Can't you see?"

The Lion told the cub, "Come with me," and took him to

a nearby pond. And then he told the cub, "Look at my face, and now look at the reflection of my face in the still pond."

The lion cub saw the majestic face of the Lion and then saw the reflection of that face in the pond. Then he saw his own reflection in the pond. He became still for a moment which felt like eternity, and then gave out a loud roar, "I am a Lion." The Universe resounded with a joyful cry. I am a Lion.

THE STORY OF THE WALLED CITY

How a Successful Man Relates to His Environment

There was a city surrounded by a wall so big that nobody could see what was outside the city. The citizens of the city could only see the sky and what was in the city.

Everyone that scaled up the straight wall and stood on top of the wall, jumped off the wall. They never came back. So nobody in the city knew what was on the other side of the wall. This got everybody curious and they wanted to find out what was there outside.

The Mayor of the City called a council meeting to find out ways and means to know what was outside the city. In the Council meeting a young man came up with a brilliant idea. He said, "If we select one of us to climb up the wall and before that person climbs the wall we should tie a rope to his feet, and when he jumps we will pull him back. This way we can find out what is there, outside the city."

Everybody clapped and gave him a standing ovation. The Council, owing to the young man's brilliance, selected him to do the job. They had their ceremony for this big occasion and they were waiting with controlled patience for all these rituals to be over with to find out what is out there.

The man scaled the wall. The whole population of the city watched with bated breath to know the truth. The man stood on top of the wall. The people below saw the man's face gleam with ecstasy. Like everyone before him, he too helplessly jumped. The city folks let out a grand cheer. He was pulled back and brought to the city square.

They asked, "Tell us, Oh our Hero what did you see?"

The people waited for the Truth. The young man became silent. He could not say anything.

When you will know the Truth, you too will become silent. There are no words in any language to express what you will experience, when you have scaled the wall of your mind through meditation, and see what lies beyond. Anything you say will only sound like gibberish to those who don't know. Silence will prevail in your life and you will live in bliss.

THE STORY
OF
TWO BIRDS

A Love Story of the Soul and the Mind

This is the story of two birds, one that was living in a golden cage and the other who was living free in the forest. Somehow by the wondrous work of the Almighty they met and fell in love.

It is a mystery what the Almighty had in Its mind.

The bird of the forest told the bird of the cage, "Come, let's fly away free to the forest together."

The bird of the cage said to the bird of the forest, "Come

stay with me in the cage, it is comforting, secure and well protected."

The bird of the forest said, "No, I will not let myself be caged and shackled."

The bird of the cage replied, "How can I go to the forest? I can't."

So the bird of the forest sat outside the cage and sang the songs of freedom of the forest. The bird of the cage sat in its golden cage and sang the songs it had been taught to sing.

"Why don't you sing the songs of the forest, the songs of freedom?" asked the bird of the forest.

"Why don't you learn the songs of the cage?" replied the bird of the cage.

The bird of the forest said, "No, I don't want to sing taught songs. I don't want to sing songs you were made to sing. I want to sing the songs of my heart."

"How can I sing songs of the forest?" asked the bird of the cage.

The bird of the forest said, "Look up at the open sky, absolutely clear blue. There are no limits anywhere."

The bird of the cage responded, "Look at this golden cage; it is furnished, neat and tidy and secure."

The bird of the forest sighed, "Let go of yourself. Release yourself amidst the clouds and spread your wings and fly with me and feel the freedom."

The bird of the cage heaved, "I am in this place of comfort, luxury and well protected where there is no trouble. Come, live with me and enjoy the security and all the comforts that go with it."

"No, I cannot live in your golden cage. There is nowhere to fly," said the bird of the forest.

The bird of the cage replied, "How can I go with you to the clouds? There is nowhere to sit on the clouds."

This is a tale of two birds that fell in love with each other but could not reconcile their feelings. They were in love but they could not be together. Between the rods of the cage they touched each other's face. They looked at each other's eyes. But one could not understand the other or convince the other of the freedom of the forest or the luxury of the cage.

They stayed alone in their own worlds and hit their wings against the cage to feel each other and to love. And with great pain, the bird of the cage, hitting its wings against the cage asked, "Come closer."

The bird of the forest, full of agony replied, "No, if I come closer the cage door might close and I won't ever be free again."

The bird of the cage with a heavy submissive sigh said, "I don't have the strength to fly."

Translation in prose form of Rabindranath Tagore's Bengali poem *Two Birds*.

My Secret Wishes

My Secret Wishes

My Secret Wishes

My Secret Wishes